WHO INVENTED HOME VIDEO GAMES?

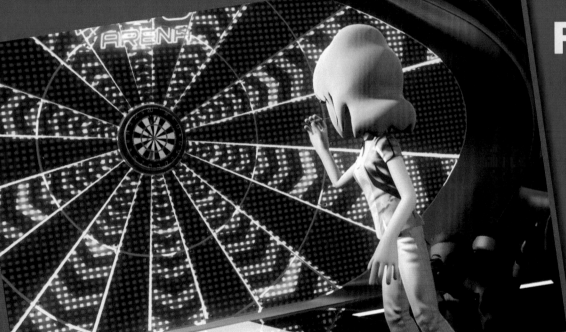

RALPH BAER

Mary Kay Carson

Enslow Elementary
an imprint of
Enslow Publishers, Inc.
40 Industrial Road
Box 398
Berkeley Heights, NJ 07922
USA

http://www.enslow.com

CONTENTS

WORDS TO KNOW 3

INVENTING FUN 5

FROM FACTORY TO FIXER 6

GAMES FOR TV 9

SECRET GAME 10

CHASING SPOTS 13

GAME MACHINE 14

POPULAR GAMES 17

MEDALS AND AWARDS 18

ACTIVITY: INVENT A GAME 20

LEARN MORE:
      BOOKS AND WEB SITES 22

INDEX 24

WORDS TO KNOW

college—A school people can go to after high school.

home video games—Games played on TVs.

invent—To make something for the first time ever.

table tennis—Game played with paddles. It is also called Ping-Pong.

White House—Where the President lives in Washington, DC.

3

INVENTING
FUN

Do you play **home video games**?
Which ones do you like most?
If you like video games, say thank
you to Ralph Baer. He **invented**
home video games.

Many people enjoy playing
video games.

FROM
FACTORY
TO FIXER

Ralph Baer was born
in Germany in 1922.

Ralph Baer moved to America when he was sixteen. His family needed money. So he worked in a factory. Then he learned to fix radios. Later he went to **college**. He learned about making TVs.

Ralph worked in a factory like this one when he was young.

Most families in the 1960s had only one TV.

GAMES FOR TV

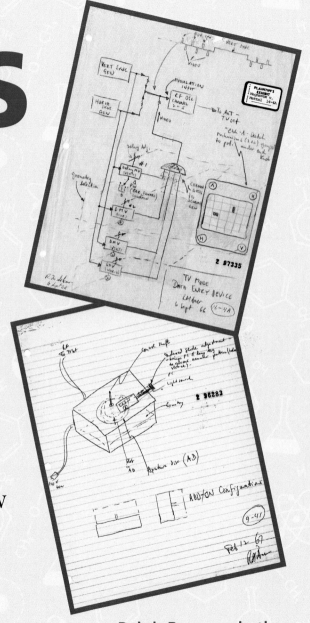

One day Baer was thinking about TV. In 1966, people just watched shows. Baer wondered what else TVs might do. What about games like soccer? Baer quickly drew a picture. It showed how a video game would work.

Ralph Baer made these drawings of his ideas.

SECRET
GAME

Baer invented the first video game with a special TV. He worked in a tiny locked room. Baer's ideas were a secret. Inventors must protect their ideas. People sometimes try to steal them.

Baer sits in front of one of his first home video games. This one is a hockey game.

CHASING
SPOTS

What was the first video game? It was a chase game. Two people played. Each player moved a spot around on the screen. The players made the spots chase each other. When one spot caught the other, that player won!

It took inventors many years to make the kinds of video games you play.

GAME
MACHINE

Baer wanted everyone to play his games. So he invented a machine. It turned a TV into a video game machine. It had simple games like **table tennis**.

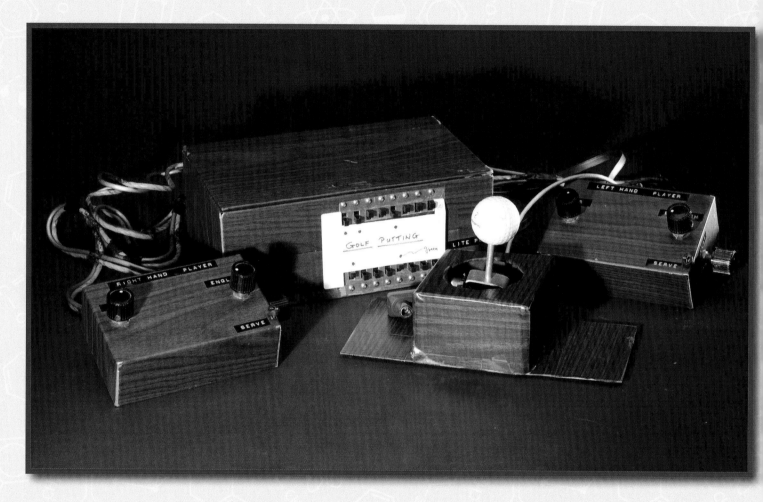

Baer built this first video game machine, called the Brown Box.
It was just the start of video games to come.

POPULAR
GAMES

Baer's invention became a big success! Baer did not stop inventing. He made other games and toys, such as Simon and Maniac. You might have played some of them.

MEDALS AND
AWARDS

In 2006, Baer went to the **White House**. President George W. Bush gave him a medal! He called him the father of home video games. So when you play video games, think of Ralph Baer.

Ralph Baer received the National Medal of Technology from President George W. Bush in 2006.

ACTIVITY: **INVENT A**
GAME

You Will Need:

- ❖ sheet of paper
- ❖ crayons or markers
- ❖ pushpin
- ❖ scissors
- ❖ index card
- ❖ foam plate
- ❖ coins or other game pieces
- ❖ tape

What To Do:

1. Draw a path of connected squares on paper. This is your game board. Write START on one end and FINISH on the other.

2. Cut off the end of an index card to make it square. Cut one end of the leftover scrap into an arrow.

3. Make a spinner: Set the square card on a foam plate. Place the arrow on top of the center of the card. Push the pushpin through both.

4. Remove the pushpin and arrow. Draw a circle on the index card around the hole. Divide it into four pie pieces. Write numbers in each from 0 to 3. Then put the spinner back together with the pushpin.

5. Invent the game! Write or draw instructions on some of the spaces. What happens when landing there? Do you lose a turn? Get to spin again? Give your game a name and decorate the board to match.

6. Play the game! Players choose markers and take turns spinning to move ahead. The first player to the FINISH line wins.

LEARN MORE

BOOKS

Boothroyd, Jennifer. *From Marbles to Video Games: How Toys Have Changed.* Minneapolis, Minn.: Lerner Publishing Group, 2011.

Jakubiak, David J. *A Smart Kid's Guide to Playing Online Games.* New York: PowerKids Press, 2010.

WEB SITES

How Stuff Works: Who Invented Video Games?
<http://science.howstuffworks.com/innovation/inventions/who-invented-video-games.htm>

Ralph Baer: Video Game History
<http://www.ralphbaer.com/video_game_history.htm>

INDEX

B
Baer, Ralph
  awards, 18
  birth, 6
  college, 6
  inventions, 5, 9, 10, 11, 13, 14, 16, 17
  jobs, 6
Brown Box, 16

Bush, George W., 18

F
factories, 6, 9

H
home video games, 5, 9, 10, 11, 13, 14, 16, 18

I
inventors, 10, 13

N
National Medal of Technology, 18

T
table tennis, 14
toys, 17
TVs, 6, 8, 9, 10, 14

W
White House, 18

Enslow Elementary, an imprint of Enslow Publishers, Inc.

Enslow Elementary® is a registered trademark of Enslow Publishers, Inc.

Library of Congress Cataloging-in-Publication Data

Carson, Mary Kay.
  Who invented home video games? Ralph Baer / Mary Kay Carson.
    p. cm. — (I like inventors!)
  Includes index.
  ISBN 978-0-7660-3975-9
  1. Baer, Ralph H.—Juvenile literature. 2. Video games—History—Juvenile literature. 3. Inventors—United States—Biography—Juvenile literature. 4. Electrical engineers—United States—Biography—Juvenile literature. I. Title.
  GV1469.3.B33C37 2012
  794.8092—dc22
  [B]   2011018039

Future editions:
Paperback ISBN 978-1-4644-0135-0
ePUB ISBN 978-1-4645-1042-7
PDF ISBN 978-1-4646-1042-4

Printed in the United States of America
012012 The HF Group, North Manchester, IN
10 9 8 7 6 5 4 3 2 1

To Our Readers: We have done our best to make sure all Internet Addresses in this book wer active and appropriate when we went to press. However, the author and the publisher have n control over and assume no liability for the material available on those Internet sites or o other Web sites they may link to. Any comments or suggestions can be sent by e-mail t comments@enslow.com or to the address on the back cover.

Series Consultant:
Duncan R. Jamieson, PhD
Professor of History
Ashland University
Ashland, OH

Series Literacy Consultant:
Allan A. De Fina, PhD
Dean, College of Education
Professor of Literacy Education
New Jersey City University
Past President of the New Jersey Reading Association

Photo Credits: © 2011 Photos.com, a division of Getty Images, pp. 2, 23; AP Images, p. 11 AP Images/Pablo Martinez Monsivais, p. 19; Archives Center, National Museum of American History, Smithsonian Institution, p. 9; Courtesy of Ralph H. Baer, Division of Medicine & Science, National Museum of American History, Smithsonian Institution, p. 16; Courtesy of Microsoft, pp. 1, 4, 12; H. ARMSTRONG ROBERTS/CLASSICSTOCK/Everett Collection, p. 8; © INTERFOTO/Alamy, pp. 15, 17; Library of Congress, Prints and Photographs, p. 7; Paul Rapson/Photo Researchers, Inc., p. 3 (home video games); Shutterstock.com, pp. 3 (college, inventor, White House), 20, 21, 22; WENN Photos/Newscom, p. 6.

Cover Photo: Shutterstock.com (controller)